Legends of the Lake

CONTENTS

Illustrations by:
Zara Merrick
Sandra Caleffi
Serena Curmi

The Enchanted Lake

An Irish Legend

Retold by ROSALIND KERVEN

There was once a prince called Donn. He was handsome, brave and helpful.
One day, a wise man who lived at the king's castle said to Donn:

Donn was puzzled, but he thanked the wise man and followed his advice.

He rode for many days, searching in vain for the lake. One day he came across an old woman. She was standing outside her cottage, crying.

Donn waded into the stream, picked some watercress and handed it to the old woman.

Donn thanked her again, jumped onto his horse and rode onwards.

Soon Donn felt hungry so he took a bite from the magic apple.

No sooner had he done so, than it grew back again, just as the old woman had promised.

He rode on for many more days and nights until, at last, he came to the enchanted lake. It was a wild and lonely place.

On the opposite side of the lake, he heard someone singing. The song sounded sweet but very mournful.

Donn walked round the lake and spied a beautiful girl on the grass. She had long, golden hair and a silver, scaly tail like a mermaid.

Well, my name is Nessa and my father is good Chief Conor. When I was a baby, this great lake did not exist. Instead our castle stood on this spot.

Near the castle was a well. It was enchanted, so we always kept a large stone on top of it.

One day I was alone in the castle. I felt thirsty and went out to the well to fetch a drink.

While I was there, I spied some butterflies. They were so beautiful, I forgot to cover the well with the stone.

There was a hissing noise. A huge, black eel came out of the well, and water spilled out in a great flood! Then the eel raised up its head – and spoke!

I shall turn this water into the biggest lake in all Ireland. Your castle will sink beneath it and your father will have to flee ...
... and I shall transform you into a mermaid. You will be doomed to live in my lake forever.
Nessa gazed at Donn in despair.
Only the death of the wizard can free me, and that is impossible.
Her eyes filled with tears. Then she dived into the water and disappeared.

Donn sat down by the lake. He waited and he thought deeply, remembering how the old woman had given him her blessing to bring him luck.

At last the sun set and night fell. The water began to ripple. There was a terrible cackling sound. A dark shape rose up from the lake. It was the eel!

Hurriedly, Donn felt in his pocket ... and pulled out the magic green pebble. By the light of the moon, he took aim.

The pebble flew through the air.

It struck the eel...

The eel screamed and fell back into the water, dead with a single blow!

Nessa swam towards Donn. She emerged from the water – and her tail fell away! Now she was a beautiful princess. Donn instantly fell in love with her at once.

Of course she was already in love with her brave hero!

Nessa and Donn decided to get married. Nessa's father, Chief Conor, gave them a wonderful wedding.

The wise man and the old woman came to celebrate with them, and Nessa and Donn lived happily ever after.

As for the lake, it's still there in Northern Ireland. It is known as Lough Neagh. But luckily it is no longer enchanted!

LOCH NESS

A Scottish Legend

Retold by GERALDINE McCAUGHREAN

In the beginning, when magic was still to be found everywhere, there was a valley. The sides were so high and steep that it looked as if giants had dug the valley with a giant axe.

Shadow filled it to the brim, like dark water. Even so, plenty of people still chose to live there.

They built their houses on the steep valley sides and descended each day to the bottom of the valley.

For there, bubbling up between the black stones, was a spring of the sweetest water in all Scotland.

The spring tasted of Sundays in May and wild strawberries. In fact, the spring-water tasted of Spring and Summer. Even in the driest weather, it never failed.

This tiny trickle of ice-cold water could fill every bucket in every house in the valley.

It washed dirty shirts and sticky faces.

It quenched everyone's thirst.

It cooked vegetables and swelled porridge oats. It never ran dry because it was magic.

The only thing to remember was the lid that rested over the spring.
Always put back the lid!
Always put back the lid!
As the years rolled by, no one remembered why it mattered, but everyone remembered to put it back.

One day, Meg took her son Robbie by the hand, and walked down to the spring. As she bent down and lifted off the lid, Robbie toddled away on his stocky little legs.

Now Robbie was brave and Robbie was clever. His hair was the colour of fire. Whenever his mother said, “No!” Robbie said, “Why?” Whenever his mother said, “Walk,” Robbie cried, “Run! Run!”

But Robbie did not stay close. He had only just learned to run, and he wanted to practise. When the wind lifted an old bird's nest and rolled it across the ground, Robbie chased it.

The ground was dark and bumpy, and the stones were sharp. But Robbie was brave and Robbie was clever … or so he thought.

Meg heard him cry out. Her heart almost spilled, like the bucket in her hand. Up she jumped and ran to find her boy. His sobs rang round the narrow valley.

The shadows were as black as ink. Big boulders crouched everywhere, like fat trolls. Meg searched and called, called and searched.

Robbie called, too:

Meg asked the crows who crouched in their black feather cloaks:

But the crows only shrieked back at her:

At last mother and baby found each other. There were specks of stone in Robbie's grazed knee. Blood trickled down like spring-water.

Meanwhile, the magic spring bubbled up like the blood, but no one ran to cover it with the lid. So the bubbling grew to a babbling. The trickle grew to a flow.

Without the magic lid to stop it, the magic spring sprang up into a fountain.

From puddle to pond, from pond to pool, the water spread out. It seemed to be lapping up the whole valley with a great silver tongue of water!

Meg scooped up her son and ran. The water overtook her; the lid washed past her as she waded uphill, but it was too late to put it back.

People and animals from end to end of the valley left their homes and gardens, and ran – up, up – towards the skyline.

Looking back, they saw no valley, only dark deeps of water, a long lake lapping and overlapping its shores.

"Tha loch nis ann!" they cried in their Celtic language. "There is a lake there now!" And that became the name of the lake: *Loch Ness*.

The magic was less strong afterwards, of course. It had been watered down a million times over. But all lakes have some magic, and Loch Ness still had more than most.

As the loch grew, so too did a creature caught in the magic flood. An ant, was it, or a slug? A worm? I don't know. But Time taught it how to swim and Magic swelled it into a monster!

From end to end of the loch it swam, a dark and dangerous shape. People spoke of it in hushed whispers.

Some said they had seen a flicker of movement out of the corner of an eye.

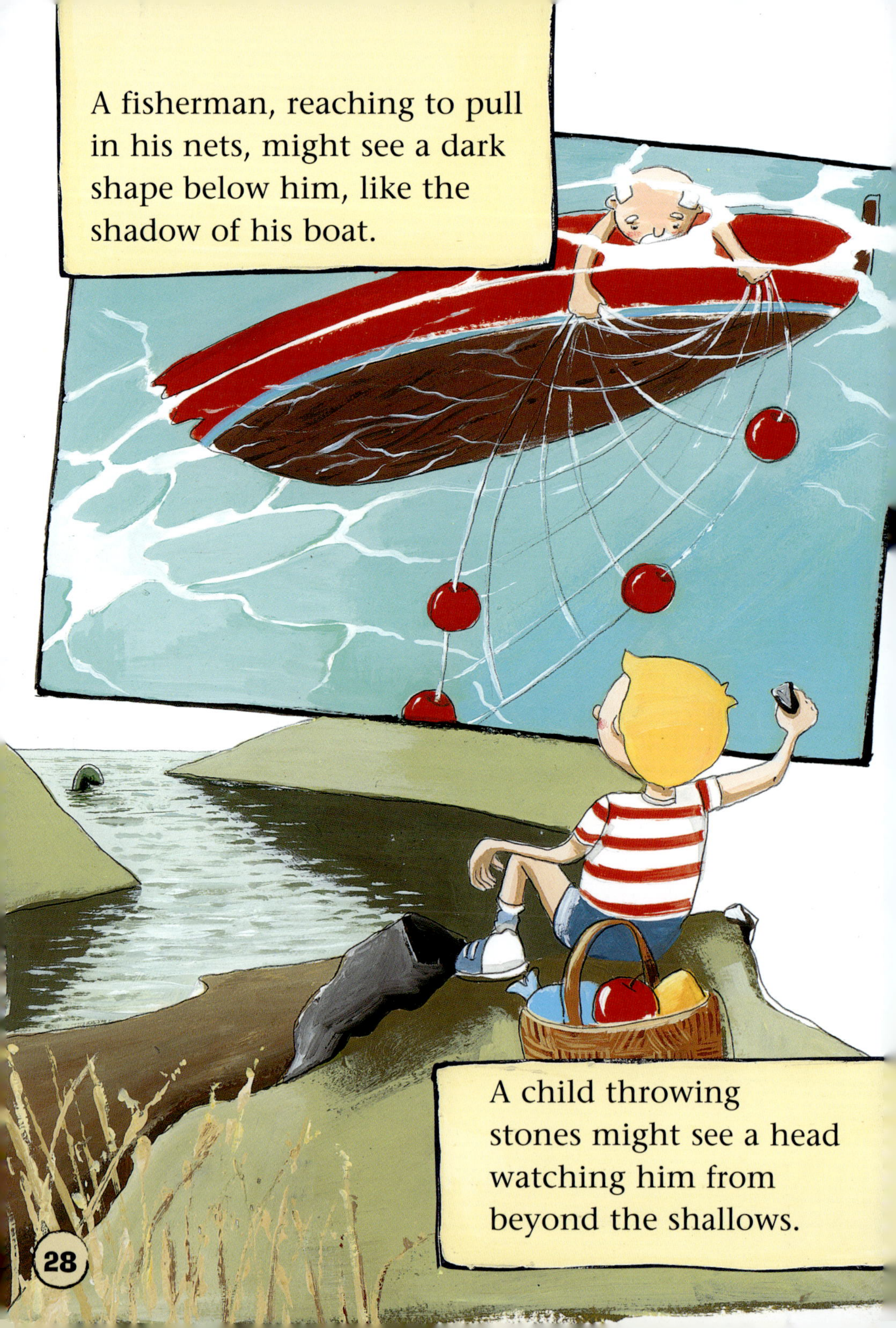

A fisherman, reaching to pull in his nets, might see a dark shape below him, like the shadow of his boat.

A child throwing stones might see a head watching him from beyond the shallows.

A swimmer might feel he was not really alone...

Over the years, stories came flooding out of the valley. Some were believed and some were not.

Divers have searched Loch Ness, scientists have studied it. Tourists have hurt their eyes staring out at its glittering waves.

Storytellers have told their stories, liars have told lies. Only the old, old hills remember how it all began. Only they know the secrets of Loch Ness.

If you are ever in the Highlands, between
Glen Garry and the sea, why don't you ask them?

THE LADY of the LAKE

A Welsh Legend
Retold by JENNY NIMMO

In the Black Mountains of Wales, there is a beautiful lake called Llyn y fan fach – Lake of the Little Place. People tell a very strange story about this lake.

The story begins with magic, but it ends with something true and wonderful; something that exists to this very day.
Long, long ago there was a shepherd called Gwyn. He lived with his mother on a farm near the town of Myddfai.

The life of a shepherd was very lonely. All day and all night, Gwyn had to guard his sheep on the wild, empty mountains. He longed for a wife, but how would he ever find one?

One day Gwyn took his sheep to graze beside Llyn y fan fach. At night he wrapped himself in a thick cloak and sat down to guard his flock. In those days wolves still lived in the mountains.

As Gwyn dozed beside a rock, he saw three ghostly figures gliding out of the lake. They began to walk through the flock of sheep.

They were women and they looked like sisters. The one who came closest to Gwyn was the most beautiful. Her golden hair floated to her waist, and her long blue dress shimmered in the moonlight.

Gwyn jumped up. He took some bread from his pocket and offered it to the woman. She smiled, took the bread and bit it.

Then she threw down the bread and ran back into the lake with her sisters. Gwyn could hear them laughing under the water. The sound was like music.

Next day Gwyn ran back to the farm to fetch a loaf of soft bread. He hurried to the lake and waited for the three women to appear.

That night, when the moon was very bright, the three sisters rose out of the water. Gwyn held out his bread. The most beautiful sister smiled, took the bread and bit it. She threw it down. Then she laughed at Gwyn and ran back to the lake with her sisters.

Gwyn had fallen in love. But the beautiful sister would only tease him. Sadly, he walked round the lake, wondering what to do.

When the sun rose he saw something floating in the water. He picked it up. It was bread. Not too hard and not too soft.
That night the three sisters appeared again. Gwyn held out the bread from the lake. The woman he loved took it.
She bit the bread and smiled.
It's good.
Stay with me and be my bride.

The lady of the lake looked at her sisters. Their eyes sparkled with mystery.

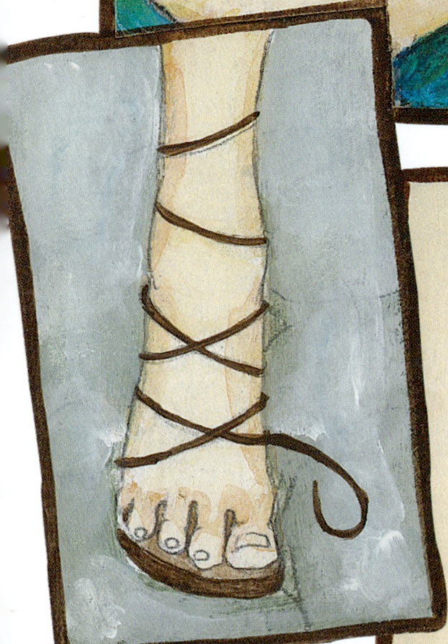

As she stepped back into the water, she tripped on a pebble. Gwyn saw that the strap of her sandal was broken.

The next night, when the three sisters appeared, it was so dark that Gwyn couldn't see their faces. He didn't know which one to choose. The women laughed at him.

He had been tricked. Then he noticed that the sister who stood nearest to him had broken the strap of her sandal.
It's you. I choose you.
They stopped laughing. Two sisters ran into the water, but the third came towards him:
Sometimes you won't understand the things I do.
I will try to be a good wife, but don't expect me to be like other women.
I'll remember.

Whatever I do, you must never strike me.
I'll never strike you.
Again she warned him.
If you strike me three times, I shall have to leave you.
It won't happen.
The Lady of the Lake turned and sang to the water. Out of the lake came three speckled cows, two grey oxen and a white bull. When Gwyn led his new bride home, the six creatures from the lake followed them.

The couple were married and lived very happily. They had three sons. The boys learned how to farm, and they also learned the ways of their mother.

Gwyn's wife grew wild herbs in a small garden behind the house. She taught her sons how to look after them, and how to cook them.

One day, Gwyn and his wife went to the church. They hadn't walked far when Gwyn's wife said:
I'm tired of walking and my hands are cold.
I'll go and look for your gloves, while you fetch the horses.
His wife agreed, but when he brought her the gloves, he found that she was daydreaming in the garden. Gwyn tapped his wife's shoulder.
You said you'd fetch the horses.
That's one.
Gwyn didn't know what she meant.

A few weeks later, the couple were invited to a wedding. In the middle of the wedding, Gwyn's wife suddenly burst into tears. Gwyn patted his wife's shoulder.
This is a happy day. Why are you crying?
Because their troubles are beginning, and so are yours. That's twice now you have hit me. The third will be the last.
For a while, Gwyn was careful never to tap his wife but several weeks later, there was a funeral. In the most serious part of the funeral, his wife started laughing. He tapped his wife's shoulder.
Hush. You musn't laugh at a funeral.
I can't help it. I warned you that my ways were different. That's three times now you've hit me. Now I shall have to leave you.

Gwyn's wife went home. She called to her cows, to the oxen and to her white bull. The bull and the cows left the meadow, and, along with the oxen, followed their mistress.

The animals followed her across the mountains until they reached the lake. There, the lady and her animals walked into the deep waters of Llyn y fan fach and vanished. Gwyn's three sons missed their mother. They couldn't understand why she had left them.

Years later, when they were young men, a terrible sickness came to the Black Mountains. People began to die and no one knew how to save them. Gwyn and his sons waited in fear for the sickness to strike them.

Then, on a cold, bright night, the three young men heard their mother's voice on the wind. It was as strong as the tug of the moon on the sea.

Wrapped in their warm capes of sheeps' fleece, they trekked over the mountains until they came to Llyn y fan fach.

Their mother stood on the shore.
It was so hard for me to leave you, but it was beyond my power to stay. I've returned to give you my secrets. They will save your lives and the lives of many others.
She gave her sons a small leather bag, full of herbs. And then she whispered her secrets so that, in the whole world, only her sons could hear them. When she had kissed them goodbye, she stepped back into the water, saying:
You are doctors now, my sons. Use my herbs in the ways I have told you and they will never fail you.

The three young men went home with their mother's herbs. Some they planted and others they crushed and mixed and boiled until they had a strong medicine.

They poured the medicine into big stone pots, and they took it to the sick and the dying.

The sick got better and the dying recovered.

After that Gwyn's three sons often went to the lake. They would call to their mother and she would come and talk to them. She gave them advice and helped them with their troubles.

The three young men became known as the Doctors of Myddfai. They passed secret recipes on to their children, and to their children's children.

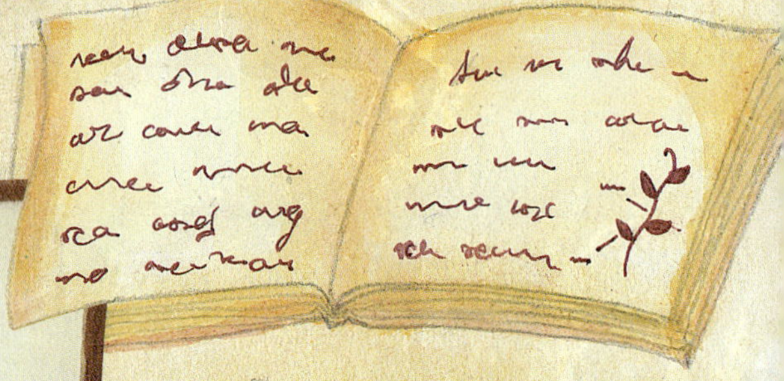

And to this very day you can still see the herbs and potions that the Doctors of Myddfai once brewed in their little house in the mountains.

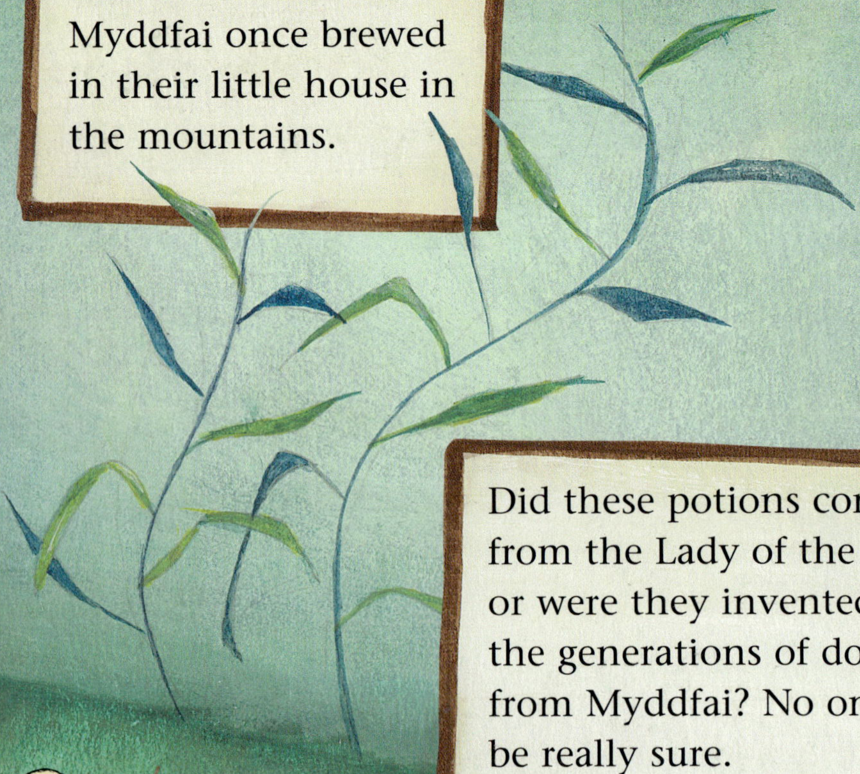

Did these potions come from the Lady of the Lake, or were they invented by the generations of doctors from Myddfai? No one can be really sure.